Million Man March

Million Man March

Text by Michael H. Cottman
Photo Editor Deborah Willis

Crown Trade Paperbacks
New York

DEDICATION

To the magnificent Black men of the Million Man March; to the millions of Black men who were not able to attend the celebration of spiritual renewal; to Black babies and Black fathers; to Black men who have collectively felt the sting of racism and who have been denied the respect you deserve, this book is for you.

To the Black men who offered their lives so that we may have a more peaceful existence; to the grandfathers and forefathers who came before us; to our African ancestors who endured years of pain and suffering but who still brought their genius to these shores, we salute you.

To Black men across the world who possess the moral fortitude to shout down bigotry and hatred, this book confirms that we are more alike than we are different, more connected than we are distant.

Be proud, be strong, and may peace be with each one of you.

FRONTISPIECE Lerone Bennett, Historian. Photo by Roy Lewis

Lines from "Strong Men" from the *Collected Poems of Sterling A. Brown*, edited by Michael S. Harper. Copyright © 1932 Harcourt Brace & Company, copyright © renewed 1960 by Sterling Brown.

Lines from "The Reverend Jesse Jackson's Speech at the Million Man March" reprinted with permission by the Reverend Jesse Jackson.

Lines from Archbishop George A. Stallings's "Prayer at the Million Man March" reprinted with permission by Archbishop George A. Stallings.

The information gathered for this book was supplemented with material from *The Washington Post*, Oct. 17, 1995; the *Final Call*, Nov. 8, 1995; *The Philadelphia Sun*, Oct. 22, 1995; and *The Philadelphia Tribune*, Oct. 20, 1995.

Published by Crown Trade Paperbacks,
201 East 50th Street, New York, New York 10022.
Member of the Crown Publishing Group.
Random House, Inc. New York, Toronto,
London, Sydney, Auckland

CROWN TRADE PAPERBACKS and colophon
are trademarks of Crown Publishers, Inc.
Printed in the United States of America
Design by Péju Alawusa and Kelvin Oden
Produced by Marie Brown Associates
Library of Congress Cataloging-in-Publication
Data is available on request.
ISBN 0-517-88763-0
10 9 8 7 6 5 4 3 2 1
First Edition

CONTENTS

INTRODUCTION

On a blustery winter evening in 1994, more than ten thousand African-American men sat on folding chairs inside a drafty Harlem armory and answered a rallying call "For Black Men Only," by Minister Louis Farrakhan, the leader of the Nation of Islam. Another seven thousand Black men stood on snow-packed sidewalks outside the armory, their hands stuffed inside coat pockets, their wool hats pulled over their ears, forming a single line that snaked around corners and stretched for blocks. It was an unprecedented assembly, a night of peace, tight handshakes, bear hugs, and promises to remove weapons from their homes and to forever respect their women. Sitting inside a huge warehouse of a building that was jammed to the second-floor rafters with Black men, I scribbled notes on a pad for my next-day story for *New York Newsday* and realized that this was just the precursor for something much more immense.

One year later, I stood in another unprecedented gathering—the largest assemblage of Black men in United States history and the largest demonstration the nation has ever witnessed. This time there were an estimated 1.2 million African-American men who joined hands in fellowship for the Million Man March in Washington, D.C. It was a day for men to join hands and pray for peace and self-responsibility; a day for Black men to sing, to rejoice, to celebrate each other. It was a day for Black men to cry, to share their universal suffering, to strengthen their spirits, atone, and pledge to rebuild their communities.

Support for the Million Man March swelled months before the event. Minister Farrakhan, the Reverend Benjamin Chavis, Dr. Cornel West, the Reverend Jesse Jackson, the Reverend Al Sharpton, and others crisscrossed the country, meeting with Black ministers and community leaders, urging Black men to join them for a day of atonement in the nation's capital. The March garnered the support of Black radio stations across the country with Bob Law, radio talk show host and New York coordinator for the Million Man March, working the national airwaves. But beyond the most visible Black leaders, there were untold numbers of African-American men and countless African-American women who worked behind the scenes to help shape the direction of not only a march but a movement.

Two thousand photographers and print, television, and radio reporters from all over the world were assigned to cover the Million Man March. This book, with more than one hundred powerful images, chronicles an event that will be etched in the hearts of Black Americans everywhere. It is not intended to document every movement, every speaker, celebrity, or poet. Rather, it is meant to offer a remembrance of one of the most pivotal and poignant moments in American history. It is a commemorative account of African-American men who answered a call for self-examination and to reaffirm their values of family, faith, and community. Think of it as a snapshot of, perhaps, the most inspiring, spiritually uplifting, and socially profound moment of our time. Cherish and reflect on this journal, which records the natural alliance and self liberation of more than one million African-American men. Share in the celebration of a vast grassroots movement, and help preserve the spirit of the Million Man March.

PHOTOGRAPH CREDITS

All photographs included in this volume are copyrighted by the individual photographer unless otherwise stated below.

Roy Lewis: 2, 35, 42, 73, 88
Jimmy Belfon: 6
Malcolm Payne: 8, 66, 95
Brian Palmer: 12, 20, 26, 47, 49, 69, 77
Hank Sloane Thomas: 13, 39, 81
Dudley M. Brooks, copyright © The Washington Post: back cover, 14, 34, 45, 49, 74
Robert Sengstacke: 14, 18, 70, 72, 77
Kwame Brathwaite: 15, 52, 53
Ron St. Clair: 15, 34
Jacques M. Chenet: 16
Christopher Griffith: 16, 17, 58-59,
Carlton Wilkinson: 17
Roland Freeman: 18, 28
Mel Wright: 19, 87
William Carter: 19, 20, 27, 66, 67, 81
Lester Sloan: 27, 28, 29, 32, 39, 54, 65, 67, 72, 78, 85, 95
Ron Campbell: 21, 33, 48, 94
Lou Jones: back cover, 22, 33
Dwayne Rogers: 30-31, 56
Keith Jenkins, copyright © The Washington Post: 32, 45, 62, 66,
Tyler Mallory, copyright © The Washington Post: 36
Ozier Muhammad/NYT Pictures: 38

James A. Parcell, copyright © The Washington Post: 40-41, 46, 47
Nancy Andrews, copyright © The Washington Post: 50-51, 61,
David Halpin: front cover, 57
Joe Hardy: 52
Marvin Edwards: 60
Andre Lambertson: 61, 87
Annalisa Kraft: 67
Jim Belfon: 68, 80
Jason Miccolo Johnson: 71, 76
Bill O'Leary, copyright © The Washington Post: 80
Eli Reed/Magnum Photo: 82
Harlee Little: 92-93, 95
Craig Herndon, copyright © The Washington Post: 60, 86
Josanne Lopez: back cover, 94
Winston Kennedy: 94
Larry Morris, copyright © The Washington Post: back cover
Ray Lustig, copyright © The Washington Post, front cover
Gediyon Kifle: front cover

OPPOSITE

1994 Rally at Armory in Harlem, New York
Photo by Jimmy Belfon

1

THE MEN OF THE MILLION MAN MARCH

It was 4:30 A.M, Monday, October 16, 1995, and the parade of footsteps on the drizzle-damp sidewalks broke the early-morning rhythms of Washington, D.C. A massive mobilization of African-American men, who were walking to prayer, was beginning to take shape in the predawn darkness—Black men whose footsteps were strong and steady, footsteps that multiplied by the minute. Footsteps with direction.

Footsteps that just kept coming.

The autumn chill was barely noticed by the more than one million African-American men who wrapped themselves in the warmth of strength, racial pride, and solidarity. These Black men temporarily altered the daily pace of the nation's capital but forever changed the social and racial perspective of a country.

They came from South Central Los Angeles and South Carolina; from Brooklyn and Birmingham; from Detroit and Cleveland, Atlanta, and Charlotte; from Oakland and Newark; from Boston, Pittsburgh, Chicago, Houston, and Miami. They came from Little Rock and Cincinnati; from Baltimore and Dallas; from Jacksonville and Jackson; from Greensboro and Anchorage, St. Paul and St. Petersburg, and Murfreesboro and Memphis.

It was a day when the world witnessed the largest gathering of African-Americans in the history of the United States. It was a day when 2.2 million people watched the monumental event unfold on television—more people than watched the Pope's address or any of President Clinton's speeches in 1995.

The marchers reflected the diversity of our nation—they were laborers and educators, postal workers and truck drivers, policemen and attorneys, waiters and electricians, ministers and businessmen, doctors and government employees, mechanics and chefs, administrators and artists, pharmacists and entertainers, athletes and politicians—fathers, husbands, brothers, uncles—all Black men telling the nation that they will take responsibility for the social despair in their communities—each of them telling the nation that he will help reduce Black-on-Black crime, respect Black women, and seek spiritual support and guidance.

And the footsteps kept coming.

It was a day of peace and spontaneous embraces, a day of reflection and self-examination, a day to pause and pray, a day to speak up and speak out against racism, a day for African-American men to honor one another; a day to remind ourselves that we're not alone.

And for some, it was a day for tears.

Like the young brother who was confined to a wheelchair, paralyzed as the result of a drive-by shooting; he cried because he couldn't walk with the throng of African-American men. Then

OPPOSITE
Black men from all over the country converged on the 22-block Mall between the steps of the U.S. Capitol and the Washington Monument.

Malcolm Payne

 9

someone picked him up and held him high over the heads of the Black men, and passed him from hand to hand across a bridge of Black shoulders.

Like the young brother who missed a bus back home. He sat alone teary eyed for only a few minutes when a group of Black men he had never met took up a collection for an airplane ticket and sent him to the airport.

Like the young brother who was scolded by a group of Black men for arguing with a police officer. He was carried four blocks from the March and told to stay away, that he was not welcome unless he changed his behavior, that he was going to ruin the spirit of the Million Man March and spoil a day of peace for over one million Black men.

African-American men shook hands, hugged and greeted the brothers standing next to them—brothers they may never see again but will never forget.

Winston Williams III, a magazine publisher from Milwaukee, stood atop a giant plant holder and shook every hand that came his way. "I'm just caught up in the mood, the movement of our people," Williams said. "I'm just feeling good about being Black; ain't no fighting, no cursing, just feeling good about being Black."

"I remember Martin Luther King's march, but there is something about the unity and feeling among Black men that makes this different," said Woody Henderson, an interior designer from New York. "I already see brothers walking taller."

Lawrence Auls, a mortgage banker from Columbus, Ohio, said, "What we have done today is respected the differences, acknowledged the differences, but we also found the common ground that we needed to be here."

"It's time to get our act together," said Sam Ewell, a barber from Newport News, Virginia. "This is about self and community. Especially if you're living in the Black community, you can see the devastation that is occurring; drugs and homelessness and illiteracy and one-parent households. Hopefully, this can unify us and keep us moving forward."

Said Shanuelle Armstrong, project specialist for the National League of Cities, "It's possible for Black men to come together and unite as one without any incidents happening. I was really appreciative of the respect of the brothers. I expected a lot of men to be out there, but it's such a diverse turnout. You can see brothers from the 'hood, brothers in pin-striped suits, brothers in college, brothers uptown, brothers downtown, and they go beyond class lines to come together."

And the footsteps kept coming.

Sylvester Brown, who attended the march on Washington in 1963, brought his son, Nigel, to the Million Man March, because he wanted his son to witness how thousands of Black men could stand together.

"My being here has less to do with Farrakhan and more to do with my own personal needs," said Brown, a resident of Washington, D.C., and a police officer. "This event is larger than Farrakhan and everybody else. It's about Black men bonding with Black men and being excited about doing something positive with their lives."

"I have been to Washington, D.C., for several large rallies," said Ron Lockett, a Detroit youth counselor, "and this is, by far, the largest. They just don't want us to have this event as the largest gathering in history in the nation's capital. And they certainly don't want it to be something that can be attributed to Minister Farrakhan. No matter how many of us came to the March, I expected the number to be lowered."

"It feels good looking at so many Black people, especially brothers," said Richard Martin, who works for a Queens, New York, alarm system company. "I hope that young brothers stick together and realize that it's not about self, but about unity. It's important that we show America that we can be unified."

And the footsteps kept coming.

"It was a special moment of rare epiphany for men who have endured the effects of chattel slavery, racism, and humiliation, who have been pushed to the margins of society, bruised by an ensemble of negative stereotypes, alienated from affection and respect, and, for the most part, rendered invisible," said Herb Boyd, co-editor with Robert Allen of *Brotherman* and a resident of New York City.

"But for this brief, affirming moment, we were not invisible and isolated in our own despair but asserting our manhood for all the world to see in the nation's capital," Boyd said. "The feeling of camaraderie and euphoria moved through the massive throng like electricity. That White America was reportedly trembling in anxiety is understandable, given the potential power emanating from such unity."

"When I loooked at the sea of Black male humanity, I was overwhelmed," said Larry Bivins, a Washington correspondent for *The Detroit News*. "It was exhilarating and reassuring. It was a show of mutual love and solidarity."

And the footsteps kept coming.

Tom Feelings, a Brooklyn-born artist who recently published *The Middle Passage*, a book of powerful black-and-white art on the slave trade, arrived in Washington from his home in Columbia, South Carolina, and witnessed carloads of Black men saluting and waving to one another on the way.

"It was obvious that we needed to come together to see brothers who looked like us, brothers who didn't fit the profiles of gangsters and criminals."

"Those kinds of negative images almost lead you to believe that there are more of them than us. I searched the dictionary and there are ninety words that have negative meanings for the word 'black.'"

"Society has been so conditioned that when people hear the word 'black,' they think negative, so when people heard that one million Black men were coming together, these people, who have been preprogrammed, thought negative—but they saw something positive," Feelings said. "They saw Black men smiling. There was no drinking. Young people were courteous, attentive, and respectful. Brothers came together because they felt a need to bond."

And the footsteps kept coming.

"Buy Black, my brothers!" one young man shouted into the crowd. "Buy Black today!"

"This gathering is a mighty rejection of Black male death in every single guise and a soaring affirmation of the redemptive potential of Black men loving and learning from and listening to one another," said Michael Eric Dyson, author and Director of the Institute of African-American Studies at the University of North Carolina at Chapel Hill.

"We need to continue to embrace one another; we need to continue to reach across class lines and think about how we function among other Black men," Dyson said. "We need to discuss ways for executives and CEOs to continue embracing blue-collar Black men. We need to pay constant attention to spiritual renewal. African-American men have a great hunger for the camaraderie, fellowship, and love of other Black men.

"There is no denying that this was not a civil rights march. It was a march for spiritual renewal and psychic uplift. It was a cultural ritual of spiritual transformation, a rehabilitation of our image, and a way of bonding together to support one another as we endure the pain of Black male existence," Dyson said.

"I felt fortunate to be there to photograph the hundreds of thousands of Black men marching quietly to the Mall, past the Supreme Court, and down East Capitol Street," said Roy Lewis, an African-American photographer who continues to work for the Black press after more than thirty years. "There was a religious tone and spiritual element, throughout the day. I hear people everywhere saying that they've noticed a difference in people's attitudes after the March."

And the footsteps kept coming.

"What we did will probably never be repeated," said Omar Reynolds of West Philadelphia. "People tried to discourage us from coming, but this was about solidarity and being proud to be African-American. I know I came away with a new feeling of love and respect for my African-American brothers."

"The Black man has been belittled, ridiculed, mocked, stripped of his manhood," said Walter Guthrie, a Port Authority police officer from Laurelton, New York. "This march is an atonement for us and between men and women, to show we respect them. Let them know we're there for them and also ask them to be here for us because we also need to be appreciated."

Clem Richardson, a deputy metropolitan editor at the *New York Daily News*, said, "It was about looking inward at ourselves, what we are, what we have become...and what we can do to be better people and help build Black communities."

"We want to inspire ourselves to go back to our communities and show our sons that we can do for ourselves," Anthony Allen, who traveled with three busloads of fathers and sons from Knoxville and Oakridge, Tennessee, told the *Final Call*.

For Wilbert Bacon, the Million Man March was one of the most memorable events of his life. He took the eleven-hour bus trip to Washington and fasted along the way. His was one of eighteen buses that rolled out of Detroit, the streets lined with Black women waving and cheering the men as they rounded the corner onto the highway. He met his son, Steven, a television engineer, at the March.

"The people I met were like next-door neighbors that I've known for years. I met one brother from South Carolina; we talked for hours. I don't even remember his name, but I won't forget him. I was standing among a million Black men," Wilbert said softly. "There were no strangers."

And the footsteps kept coming....

Brian Palmer

Posters urging men to join the Million Man March were posted throughout Washington, D.C.

And some men came in wheelchairs to experience the brotherhood and bonding at the March.

Many of the men walked to the Million Man March from buses parked at RFK Stadium, from Union Station, and some even walked from as far away as Philadelphia, Pennsylvania.

▼

Fruit of Islam
lock arms on the
steps of the
U.S. Capitol.

Dudley M. Brooks, The Washington Post

Danger:
Educated Black
Man.

Kwame Brathwaite

Actor
Malik Yoba

◄ The Reverend
Al Sharpton of
New York and
D.C. Mayor
Marion Barry
looking at the
crowd gathered
at the Mall.

Robert Sengstacke

Ron St. Clair

Actor/activist
Jim Brown and
Dr. Cornel
West.

Dreadlocked
brothers at the
March.

Young brothers enjoying the March.

Carlton Wilkinson

Christopher Griffith

Sitting on the wall of the Capitol.

Brothers in
traditional
dress.

Dr. Leonard Jeffries

Participants gather on the wall in front of the Capitol.

Early call for
Fruit of Islam.

Activist/author Dick Gregory being interviewed at the March.

In the early-morning hours, in front of the Capitol, March organizer Reverend Benjamin Chavis being interviewed.

Men hold up the number one, after announcement that one million men were in attendance.

2

THE AGENDA

One thing they cannot prohibit—
The strong men . . . coming on
The strong men . . . gittin' stronger
Strong men . . .
Stronger . . .
From the poem "Strong Men"
by Sterling Brown

At that first rally in Harlem in 1994, I was awed not only by the large number of Black men who showed up on that snowy evening, but how everyone sat attentively until 11 P.M., nodding periodically when Farrakhan urged Black men to stop abusing their women and ambushing their brothers, to take responsibility in their homes and communities, to join a church, and to stimulate economic growth by supporting Black businesses.

There was no talking, no smoking, no laughter. And when Farrakhan asked every Black man to stand and greet one another, there was a simultaneous outpouring of love and respect that stunned almost everyone in the hall.

On October 16, 1995, there was a Black man in every seat aboard the diesel-fueled buses that rolled into Washington, D.C., from every corner of the country. Staking out positions along the twenty-two blocks of lawn between the United States Capitol and the Washington Monument, over one million men, a group that stretched for as far as the eye could see, gathered to listen to more than fifty speakers and to send a message to America that Black men are prepared to lead by example.

The men heard from a group that included the Reverend Jesse Jackson, the Reverend Benjamin Chavis, Stevie Wonder, Rosa Parks, Maya Angelou, the Reverend Joseph Lowery, Dr. Betty Shabazz, and Mayor Marion Barry before Minister Louis Farrakhan took the podium for a two-hour speech.

Among the goals for the Million Man March were atonement for past mistakes; renewal of our commitment to respect and end the abuse of African-American women; rebuild our communities and provide unity within our homes; register eight million Black pontential voters; create an African-American development fund to support Black organizations; and create new businesses.

In a departure from the Nation of Islam's observer posture in past political elections, Minister Farrakhan said during the March that the Nation of Islam plans to spearhead a national voter registration drive in the Black community. Some political pundits have already said that a voter registration drive of this magnitude could have a profound impact on the nation's political landscape.

"Nobody else could have led such a march," said Representative Kweisi Mfume, a Democrat from Maryland. "I'm

OPPOSITE
Young men waving the Black Liberation flag in front of the Capitol.
Lou Jones

 23

glad Minister Farrakhan told the men to get involved in politics, their communities, and Black organizations. We will now see real change in this country."

"The idea of a Million Man March has touched a nerve deep in the heart of people yearning to be free," the Reverend Jesse Jackson told the cheering crowd of Black men amassed on the Mall.

"From the U.S. Capitol, I looked toward the monument and felt a sense of pride and respect that I will never forget," said Eugene Niles, a computer analyst from Chicago, who said he would have never made it to the March if not for the assistance of a Black female reservationist with a major airline. "For me, the significance of this march versus the civil rights march of 1963 is that our fathers marched in 1963 for an equal place in our society; this march was for the economic and political survival of the Black man of today."

African-American men have reached a crossroads in American history where the constant barrage of negative images forced us to prove the skeptics wrong. We were inexplicably drawn to Washington as if we had all spoken with one another during a cross-country conference call.

The Million Man March was a day-long testament: no Black man needs to be alone in his quest for self-responsibility and self-respect. During the March we renewed our commitment to our families and communities and vowed not to allow a racially hostile society to distract us from repairing our socially and economically damaged neighborhoods.

With an assembly many times greater in number than those who listened to Martin Luther King deliver his "I Have a Dream" speech in 1963, the Million Man March was the beginning of a social movement, one that garnered the same kind of intensity and passion as did the civil rights demonstrations of the 1960s.

"There are still two Americas—one Black, one White, separate and unequal," Farrakhan said during his speech. "We are gathered here today...to move toward a more perfect union with God. We're not here to tear down America...We're here to rebuild the wasted cities."

There was silence for the speakers as the crowd listened attentively to every word spoken. During Maya Angelou's poignant poem, "From a Black Woman to a Black Man," she shouted, "Clap hands," and Black men responded instantly with the thunder of Black hands slapping together.

When asked to show economic solidarity by waving a single one-dollar bill in the air, one million Black men, without hesitation, reached into their pockets and pulled dollars —and tens and twenties—from their wallets and waved them in a sincere display of unity that few had ever seen before.

If there was one defining moment during the fifteen-hour event, one moment that captured the hearts of a million Black men and the attention of a nation, it was when Black men joined hands and in unison recited a solemn pledge: "I pledge that from this day forward, I will never raise my hand with a knife or gun to beat, cut, or shoot any member of my family or any human being except in self-defense."

"There's a new Black man in America today," the Reverend Benjamin Chavis, an organizer of the Million Man March, said during an interview. "This new Black man is upright, respectful, and diligent. The Million Man March was more than a one-day event, the spirit of the Million Man March is still alive in cities all across this country. It defied the stereotypical negative images of African-American men...They showed a sense of admiration for one another and a sense of discipline. This is the new Black man."

Why did we march?

We marched against stereotypes. We marched against media that continue to portray Black men as criminals. We marched against conservative ideology that is anti-Black. We marched against angry White males who have concocted a myth that Black men are taking jobs away from them through affirmative action. We marched against the Contract with America. We marched against Rush Limbaugh, Newt Gingrich, and Jesse Helms. We marched against *The Bell Curve*. We marched to silence the skeptics.

But we also marched for ourselves.

The day of the March was a day I decided to speak to every African-American man who crossed my path. It was a day that I decided to shake as many hands as I could along the way. It was a day for me to reflect on personal and professional decisions, to thank God for bringing together hundreds of thousands of brothers from diverse backgrounds. It was a day for me to rejoice and share in the celebration of Black men who spoke to one another about their goals and aspirations for themselves, as well as their children.

As throngs of African-American men gathered that morning at the foot of the United States Capitol steps, fathers with their sons on their shoulders, Black men with X caps, Black men with suits and ties, Black men wearing colorful African robes, Black gay men, Black men with headsets listening to the speeches, Black men with poetry they brought to share, Black men with smiles, I witnessed a rite of passage unfold before me. By midday, the Mall was awash in banners, African-American flags, signs of faith and hope, and Black clenched fists raised in the air—a stark contrast to the humiliation and inhumane treatment that Blacks were forced to endure some 300 years ago. Black men, swelled with pride, seemed to stretch for miles in front of the white marble, colonial-era monuments. I witnessed a day of brotherhood—a peaceful, polite show of affection between Black men—a day where the pundits, statisticians, and political analysts could only offer generic interpretations because although they witnessed the March, they were not of it.

I was struck by the spontaneous outpouring of affection, camaraderie, solidarity, and complete, absolute trust from so many African-American men who answered a call and who broke the unspoken class barriers that divide us daily: the corporate attorneys who embraced the unemployed, the businessmen who hugged the homeless; men who followed their hearts—not necessarily their leaders—to bond with Black men they had never met before, during a day that, perhaps, we will never witness again.

I watched a young brother lead a blind man through a crowd that parted within seconds to create an unobstructed path. The blind man whispered of a spiritual presence that he could feel but not see.

I felt embraced by the hearts of a million Black men whose unbridled power seemed to shake the earth beneath my feet. I felt sheltered from all criticism while weaving my way through the maze of Black men as if I had reached my personal Promised Land after a long, tiring journey.

In a spiritual sense, I was at home.

Brian Palmer

**Dr. Conrad Worrill
of the National
Black United Front**

According to Boston University's center for Remote Sensing, the National Park Service overlooked hundreds of thousands of Black men under the trees as a result of bad angles from aerial photographs, and estimated the crowd at somewhere between 870,000 and 1.1 million. Psychologist Dr. A.J. Franklin said the manipulation of numbers is an aspect of "deep denial. This is merely another attempt to keep us invisible," he explained. "You have to understand that it was an ever-shifting crowd, but it maintained density throughout."

"There were anecdotes, from Black Americans, about this society's inability to tell the truth and see Black men, about how it may be that the society was still holding to the idea that we are only three-fifths of a man," said Herb Boyd, co-editor of *Brotherman*.

One Million Men
—One God.

William Carter

Fruit of Islam on the steps of the U.S. Capitol. Photo by Lester Sloan

Unique view of ▶
the Mall.

Hear our voices ▼
U.S.A.

Lester Sloan

Lester Sloan

Roland Freeman

Million Man Marchers from Detroit.

"Let freedom ring."—Martin Luther King

PREVIOUS PAGES
Historical presence.
Photo by Dwayne Rogers

ABOVE
**When asked to
contribute $1 each,
one million Black men
reached into their
pockets and waved
dollar bills.
Photo by Keith Jenkins,
*The Washington Post***

RIGHT
One hand—one dollar.

Lester Sloan

Gentleman of
the March.

Lou Jones

The Reverend
Jesse Jackson
and Rock
Newman

Ron Campbell

A salute of
support.

Singing the
Memphis blues.

OPPOSITE
The face of the
Million Man March
—harmony, love
and power.
Photo by Roy Lewis

3

THE JOURNEY AND ARRIVAL

Thousands of people prepared Washington, D.C., for the Million Man March: A Black-owned Internet consulting firm in Virginia provided on-line subscribers with the latest information about the March and some seven hundred Black medical and emergency professionals manned first-aid stations.

Five hundred Black lawyers and paralegals monitored the crowd; hundreds of young men pushed wheelbarrows filled with ice water; hundreds of vendors sold food; and Black off-duty police officers patrolled the crowd.

Busloads of Black men from coast to coast packed brown-bag lunches, waved good-bye to their families, and headed off into history. They traveled to Washington, D.C., from every corner of the country. They came by bus, van, car, train, and airplane. Sixty-two Black men even walked from Philadelphia.

"It took us eleven hours, six minutes, and seventeen seconds to get here," Ron Robinson from Lansing, Michigan, told the *Final Call*, the official newspaper of the Nation of Islam. "It was wonderful being on the road and seeing so many cars, vans, and buses filled with brothers that were coming from everywhere."

Norman L. Thomas told the *Final Call* that he reflected during his Greyhound trip to Washington from Alabama. "As I sat there and rode that bus, I thought about the freedom rides, Emmitt Till, and the march on Selma as we were riding making stops in Georgia, South Carolina, and Virginia, picking up brothers along the way."

Cars packed with Black men honked horns on the interstate highways as young men stuck their clenched fists through the sunroofs of cars in a show of solidarity. Young Black men wore Million Man March caps and T-shirts that read, "Yes, I'm Black—No, I'm Not a Criminal."

Mark Stephens, a singer and hairstylist, drove to Washington with five friends. From the moment he arrived at the March, he knew he was among a million acquaintances. "It was great to spend a day with so many brothers from all over the country," Stephens said. "It was a positive day; none of the stereotypes we always read about. Now it's time to make a difference. We have an obligation to look after the young people in our communities, police our own neighborhoods, and exercise our right to vote."

Wendell Moore, a member of the Greater Germantown Turn It Over—a Philadelphia-based drug and alcohol rehabilitation facility—laced up his sneakers and walked from Philadelphia to Washington with sixty-one other African-American men in the program. It took them four days to cover the 120 miles, stopping at colleges and churches to sleep. Their route: the path of the Underground Railroad.

"This march was long overdue," Moore said. "We rewrote history with this march and I wanted to be a part of it. I marched for all those brothers who could not be a part of it. I let the younger brothers know that this march is for the next generation of brothers, that the struggle is far from over. I told them they should all get involved in this movement."

Michael Tucker, a lecturer at Howard University, did not have to travel a long distance to the march, but experienced it as a psychic journey: "Since the March, I walk taller, I hold my head higher, and I'm less concerned with what Whites think, because I truly believe the only validation I need comes from my Creator and my people. I believe the Creator blessed the gathering because my son, Chris, deserves a world filled with loving men and women who look like him."

Andre Gadson, greeted by the Reverend Ra Kabeer on bus to Washington from Atlanta.

Hank Sloane Thomas

Brotherhood and bonding at the March.

Walkers from
Philadelphia.

Lester Sloan

FOLLOWING PAGES
Fruit of Islam at 3:30 in
the morning.
Photo by James A. Parcell,
The Washington Post

4

TOGETHER IN PRAYER AND SONG

The sun had burned off the morning mist, warming the hearts of the patient Black men who were gathered along the twenty-two-block Mall where Archbishop George A. Stallings, founder of the Imani African-American Catholic Congregation, delivered the opening prayer to Protestants, Catholics, Muslims, and those of other faiths, to the rich and the underprivileged, the young and the old, the fit and the frail.

He asked Black men to join hands while he offered his prayer. As the brothers listened to Archbishop Stallings's masterly message, some holding joined hands high in the air, tears streamed from the eyes of many of the men, some of them crying for the first time since childhood, each of them rejoicing.

"We pray as Black men, give us strength to put down our guns and pick up our babies. Help us to put away the crack and CLEAN UP OUR ACT! Help us to check ourselves before we wreck ourselves!" Stallings prayed in a hushed silence. "We promise you, today, O God, that we are going to return to our homes as committed Black men to change our communities, our families, and ourselves."

Stallings was one of the many pastors and religious leaders from a multitude of denominations who came together for the Million Man March to offer peace and hope to the African-American men who stood before them. There were Catholic priests, Muslim ministers, and Protestant pastors who led more than one million Black men in one universal day-long prayer. Spiritual leaders who attended included: Minister Abdulla Muhammad of Mosque Maryan; the Reverend Clay Evans from Chicago; the Reverend Al Sharpton, the Reverend Wyatt Tee Walker, and the Reverend Johnnie Ray Youngblood of New York; the Reverend Wendell Anthony, the Reverend William Reverly, Jr., and the Reverend Frank Madison Reid from Baltimore; Bishop H. H. Brookins from Los Angeles; the Reverend Fred Haynes from Dallas; and Islamic Sheikh Ahmed Tijani of Ghana.

"It was overwhelming for me to hear the brother singing the prayer al-Fatehah, the opening sura in the holy Koran, in Arabic over the public address system. Witnessing the largest gathering of African descendants in the history of this nation, all standing tall before Allah, asking to be shown the Straight Way, was the most powerful feeling I've ever experienced," said Hank Jennings, a database designer in Miami. "Millions of African people brought to these shores were Muslim. It seems ironic that we've come full circle, asking for atonement in an Arabic song of prayer, in a religion that had a familiar feel to it. I will always carry that moment from the Million Man March in my soul."

After the March, Archbishop Stallings said, "When preparing the prayer for the Million Man March, I thought of ways to connect with one million Black men; to touch on those issues that affect the quality of life of African-American people and particularly the Black male experience in America. I felt that I must somehow touch the spiritual fiber of these African-American men and not offer them just another prayer but establish a spiritual communion, to touch them spiritually and collectively and bind them in a sense of brotherhood and togetherness—all in three minutes.

"I decided on faith as a theme. If there is any one element that has held the Black American community together, it has been faith," Archbishop Stallings continued. "There is an old song that goes 'We've come this far by faith, leaning on the Lord, trusting His holy word, He hasn't failed us yet.' The staying power for us as a people is faith. We've endured slavery, hardship, racism, discrimination, and we still hold our heads up high with the blessed assurance that the Lord will make a way for us somehow. We are the quintessential expression of faith, and that is why that good feeling and goodwill spread through all those Black men throughout the entire day of the Million Man March. They were held together by spiritual roots, by self-determination to take ownership, and control of their own destiny.

"The Million Man March came along at the right time," Stallings said. "There was a serious vacuum, a valley of despair in the Black community that desperately needed addressing. Minister Farrakhan seized the day and had the vision to call for the March more than a year ago when he was gathering thousands of Black men together in major cities across this country—New York, Washington, Chicago, Los Angeles, Houston, Atlanta."

Since the days of slavery, prayer and song have served as the spiritual threads that connect our families and our lives. Prayer and song have been the two most steady components that have held us together as a people. Prayer and song lift our spirits up when we're down and provide a vehicle for thanking God when we rejoice.

"I cannot see you, but I can see your spirit, and I feel your presence," Stevie Wonder told the cheering assembly of Black men. "For every poor man born in the ghetto, for every middle-class man born in the middle, for every rich class man born rich—no matter what we may be in class, we are all one people. I love you."

"Stevie! Stevie! Stevie," the crowd had roared as the legendary musician was escorted to the microphone. Moments later, Wonder enthralled the crowd with an extemporaneous a cappella tribute of Black love, peace and hope—expressions that have become synonymous with the songwriter.

The music of the March filled the Mall from sunrise to sunset. There were drums, flutes, piccolos, tambourines, a blend of heartwarming harmonies and soulful solos. There were appearances by African drummers, the Boys Choir of Harlem, the Million Man March Chorus, the Thelonius Monk Family Ensemble, the Kankouran West African Dance Troupe, Bro Ah and the Sounds of Awareness, Melvin Deal, and the African Heritage Dancers and Drummers.

"God Is," a song that seemed to float through the mass of Black mankind, was performed by Tony Powell.

The Reverend Willie Wilson, of the Union Temple Baptist Church, lead the

Healing
prayers.

Dudley M. Brooks, The Washington Post

Keith Jenkins, The Washington Post

Keith Jenkins, The Washington Post

ABOVE
Participants pray during the service on the Mall.

RIGHT:
Praying for solidarity.

gathering in a thundering rendition of "Lift Every Voice and Sing," during which a sea of Black men swayed back and forth, waving their arms with a deliberate, synchronized style as if in a movement choreographed by the spirit of Alvin Ailey.

"This march came out of the need for spiritual renewal; it was a call for Black men to heighten their moral vision, to deepen their spiritual passion, to extend ethical inspiration of the rich traditions that produced us," said Michael Eric Dyson, a scholar and ordained minister who teaches at the University of North Carolina at Chapel Hill. "It was important for us to atone and search ourselves in the presence of God and listen to the voice of God during these difficult times of constant demands on Black men. Prayer is the only way to reclaim the vital center of our lives and our families. We need to pay more attention to the spiritual yearnings and urgings that animate human behavior, that give life to the most poignant moments and clearest meanings, and without prayer, that is impossible. Prayer gives us motivation to exercise those public principles we cherish dearly; prayer is the vital link between what we know we ought to do and what we ultimately end up doing. Prayer not only gives us the ability to move mountains, but it changes our attitudes about the mountains we face."

James A. Parcell, The Washington Post

Answered prayers.

▲ Prayers for the
million men.

◀ Joining hands.

Brother Beel pouring libation.

Brian Palmer

▲ Praying in front of
Capitol Building.

Dudley M. Brooks, The Washington Post

Musicians drumming
the message.

Standing tall.

Kwame Brathwaite

Black Catholic
Men's Summit

Joe Hardy

PREVIOUS PAGE
**Christian
Brothers United.
Photo by
Nancy Andrews,**
The Washington Post

OPPOSITE
**Stevie Wonder.
Photo by
Kwame Brathwaite**

5

OUR YOUTH / OUR FUTURE

Slight in size but towering in spirit, fourteen-year-old Ayinde Jean-Baptiste of Chicago approached the lectern at the Million Man March and preached his way into the hearts of one million men.

"When you stop making excuses, when you start standing with our mothers, when you stick it out with your family, when you start mentoring our young, when you start teaching us to be humane, then we can build a new nation of strong people," Ayinde bellowed from behind the bulletproof screen at the edge of the United States Capitol. "Then your children will not join gangs, because they belong to a community."

Despite speaking in a voice that is far from baritone, Ayinde managed to inspire African-American men five times his age. His wise words were met with rousing applause by older men and students who nodded in approval.

Tiffany Jamille Mayo, a ten-year-old girl from Waldorf, Maryland, also took her place at the podium, and read a poem by Maya Angelou, introduced by these remarks:

"Thank you for this power March. It's all for me. I represent the Black woman of the twenty-first century . . . I'm everyone's daughter and everyone's sister and everyone's friend and everyone's niece. I must count on your clean devotion to me. I am not yet a woman, even if I pretend to be; I am tender enough to curl into the palm of your hand. I need the protection of every Black man."

Milton Boyd and Bashiri Wilson of Jefferson Junior High School in Washington, D.C., read:

"Wake up, my father! Wake up, my father!" they exclaimed. "Wake up, get up, our fathers, hear and fill our needs. I need your strength. To all those that want to be called 'Pops,' I need your respect. For all those that want to be called 'Brother,' I need your courage."

Ayinde, Tiffany, Milton, and Bashiri represented the voices of the young from the Million Man March—fresh, strong, and innocent voices of the generation that will lead African-Americans through the twenty-first century; voices that need to be heard; voices that must be nurtured.

"The March represented a watershed event in the lives of a generation that has been groping for mass mobilization and mass movement," said Conrad Muhammad, who heads the Nation of Islam's Mosque #7 in Harlem, New York. "We crisscrossed the country reaching out to the youth in the African-American community and specifically appealed to them. There was tremendous representation from men thirty and under at the March. I believe that young

OPPOSITE
**Ayinde Jean-Baptiste.
Photo by
Lester Sloan**

 55

Black men are discovering that there is more to life than rap and dance clubs, that activism can be a desirable course of action today. The Honorable Minister Louis Farrakhan has assembled a cadre of young men and placed them in leadership positions. I was one of them."

"This is a million man movement for African-American empowerment that involves the mobilization of Black men and women and, particularly, Black youth," the Reverend Benjamin Chavis said. "Half of the Black men who attended the March were young Black men, Black youths, students, young grassroots activists who were going through a rite of passage.

"Indeed, there were mothers who brought their young sons; fathers who brought their sons; busloads of students from historically Black colleges; and young Black men who belonged to youth organizations, churches, and the NAACP.

"There were young men with signs boasting their cities, young men wearing baggy pants and knit caps, young men wearing dreadlocks and those with bald heads, young men with faces of purity, gang members and former gang members. These young men were clearly in awe of the enormous Black male alliance that was taking place around them."

Kevin Merida, a political correspondent for *The Washington Post* covered the March for his newspaper and took his two sons, Hamani and Darrell to see their father at work as he chronicled the event. "Growing up with many advantages, they needed to be there to see all kinds of brothers coming together and see that the popular notions of Black men—that we can't unite, that we're violent—was not who we are or what we're about," said Merida. "They could watch history unfold and see for themselves Black men offering mutual love and respect for each other.

"Darrell's immediate reaction was there may be trouble at the March," Merida said. "My son was worried about being in a large gathering of Black men. It said to me that my profession—a profession that I've practiced for many years—has done a great deal of damage to the image of Black men. So I felt it was important for my sons to be there, because they will be able to appreciate and see Black men coming together for a day of peace, love, and absolute trust."

Dwayne Rogers

Looking toward the future.

The brothers from Morehouse College.

Craig Herndon, The Washington Post

Marvin Edwards

▲ Father and sons.

◄ Chuck D, Ice T, and Prince D'Jour.

PREVIOUS PAGES
**Helping hands.
Photo by
Christopher Griffith**

OPPOSITE, ABOVE
United We Stand.

OPPOSITE, BELOW
**Young man listens to
the address at the
Million Man March.**

6

THE WOMEN OF THE MARCH

If there were one million Black men marching in Washington, D.C., then perhaps there were one million Black women who assembled the spiritual bridge for their journey.

The support of Black women for African-American men could be felt throughout the country. There was a mixture of subtle, spontaneous support and well-organized, extravagant celebration. Some Black women chose to show their support by joining groups and associations. Some called in to radio talk shows to offer words of encouragement.

Some stayed home from work to support the spirit of the mobilization of Black men. Some Black women went to work so Black men could take the day off. Others took up collections to pay for buses to Washington, D.C. Black airline personnel found space on airplanes so those from distant places could attend.

Black women came to Baltimore by the hundreds to shower with confetti men who were headed to the March. "We love you, brothers!" the women chanted, waving and cheering.

"When we left the buses at RFK Stadium, women came to the doors and waved as we walked to the Metro. It was beautiful; the spirit was tremendous," said Clinton Conner, a North Philadelphia businessman. "You could feel the love, the respect. These women didn't know us, but they knew why we were there and they were proud."

Black women—some working behind the scenes—offered their support, love and encouragement any way they could, whether one thousand miles away from D.C. or one thousand feet away from the United States Capitol.

"We are here to let the brothers know we support them and love them very much," said Kim Wade, a student at Hunter College in New York City, cradling her twenty-month-old daughter in her arms.

Josanne Lopez, a television news producer from New York, said she did not attend the March in protest, but simply wanted to observe the spiritually uplifting movement.

"I thought it was important to be present, to bear witness to this historic alliance of Black men, because I felt that this was the beginning of a movement for change and spiritual growth in our communities," Lopez said. "I felt that what transpired here will have a profound effect on the future of all Black men and women in America. We need to see them here, and we also needed to symbolize what they left at home. We want to be a witness to that which was promised here today."

Tanya Johnson said that she attended the March for the men in her family who were not able to be there.

OPPOSITE
Young woman overcome by words spoken at the March. Photo by Keith Jenkins, *The Washington Post*

"There are men in my family who did not come, because they were afraid to come," she said. "They were afraid of societal backlash. But this is a historic occasion, and I want to do a photojournalist's piece to show them what happened here today." Women had been asked not to attend the March, to stay home and pray and teach their children the values of self-esteem and family unity. But women who did attend the March—about 1,500 by the organizers count—ranged from teachers to students to homemakers to federal workers. Some came with friends, some with their husbands, some came alone and some women brought their sons. Several said they had attended the 1963 civil rights march on Washington as children and wanted to continue a legacy of activism.

Charlita D. Anderson, an assistant prosecuting attorney from Ohio, told *The Washington Post* that she wanted to see Black men standing strong and dedicating themselves to taking more responsibility. She said that some women are troubled because some men have not kept their promises for child support.

"I needed this for me," said Anderson, a single mother raising a seven-year-old son. "I look at this crowd and I see hope. In the future, if I think of speaking negatively of his father, I'll stop—I want my son to grow up a strong man."

The voices of women could also be heard from the podium, including Dr. Betty Shabazz, widow of Malcolm X, and Rosa Parks, considered the mother of the modern civil rights movement. Mrs. Parks, who lives in Detroit and endorsed the March from its inception, believed the moment was a good opportunity for all men, "but primarily men

of African heritage to make a change in their lives for the better," she said.

"I have waited for this day all my life, to see our brothers, our uncles, our husbands, our friends, come together as a family and take responsibility for repairing our home life, our social order, our community, and our nation," said Tynnetta Muhammad, wife of the Honorable Elijah Muhammad, founder of the Nation of Islam. "We have come to the fulfillment of a great prophecy in which Almighty God, Allah, His Spirit, has moved among the people to bring you here in this central place in Washington, D.C.; that no longer will there be a slave and slave master mentality."

Dr. Dorothy Height, the president of the National Council of Negro Women, Inc., and Queen Mother Moore also spoke. Poet Maya Angelou recited her poem, "From a Black Woman to a Black Man," written especially for the occasion of the March.

The women called on Black men and women to work as partners in dealing with social and economic problems.

"I understand that the brothers wanted this day of reckoning, they wanted an opportunity to stand up as men, first and foremost," said Gettye Israel. "I respect that because for so long, sisters have had to bear the burden and be everything to the Black family. I would say to those who are offended, be not offended, because all of this is about us."

By all accounts, African-American men embraced the women who attended the March. From helping female press members scale the Mall wall to stepping aside to allow women access to the front of the masses, the men of the Million Man March provided a tone of inclusion for women of all ages.

"This is the prettiest scene I have seen in my whole life," said Cora Masters Barry, wife of D.C. Mayor Marion Barry, as she gazed at the thousands of Black men amassed from the Capitol Building to the Washington Monument. "And I want to say to all the sisters who could not be here in spirit and prayer…that we must lift up our brothers."

Lester Sloan

The Women at pre-rally event.

Dr. Betty Shabazz,
Mrs. Rosa Parks,
and Khadijah Farrakhan.
Photo by
Malcolm Payne

Queen Mother Moore and
Dr. Delois Blakely.
Photo by William Carter

Woman praying.
Photo by Keith Jenkins,
The Washington Post

Lester Sloan

Dr. Dorothy Height

William Carter

Two members of the Vanguard.

Annalisa Kraft

Women supporters at Union Temple Baptist Church.

Annalisa Kraft

Woman in pulpit.

7

EXPRESSIONS OF WISDOM AND SOLIDARITY

EXCERPTS FROM THE REVEREND JESSE JACKSON'S SPEECH

How good it is to hear the sounds of chains and shackles breaking from the ankles and minds of men. How beautiful it is to see the rejected stones stand up, become the cornerstones of a new spiritual and social order. And to Minister Farrakhan and that host executive committee that worked so diligently to bring this march into being, let's give them a tremendous, loving, respectful round of applause.

In the spirit of atonement, we pray to God to forgive us for our sins and the foolishness of our ways as we seek to do better and never become bitter and let nothing, nobody, stand between us and the love of God. The idea of a million men has touched a nerve deep in the hearts of people yearning to breathe free. Big meetings were never allowed on the plantation. We've always yearned for a big meeting. Today, we've left the plantation. This is a big meeting. Raw nerves of ancient longing for dignity have been touched.

America will benefit and ultimately be grateful for this day. When the rising tide of racial justice and gender equality and family stability lifts the boats stuck at the bottom, all boats benefit.

Why are we here today? Because we're attacked by the courts, legislatures, mass media. We're despised. Racists attack us for sport to win votes. We're under attack for sport to make money. But I tell you, today, rabbit hunting ain't fun when the rabbits stop running and start fighting back. . . .

We've come here today because there is a structural malfunction in America. It was structured in the Constitution and they referred to us as three fifths of a human being, legally. There's a structural malfunction. That's why there's a crack in the Liberty Bell. There's a structural malfunction; they ignored the Kerner Report. Now we have the burden of two Americas: one half slave and one half free. Lincoln said it could not exist.

Why was the reaction to the O.J. verdict so different? Because there were wounds unhealed. There was more bile and venom toward the integrated jury that voted unanimously than toward the racist policeman who perjured himself. Why did Blacks and Whites see it so differently? One man standing up, looking down on an apple sees red and that which is delectable. Another man standing on the bottom, looking up sees rot and sees worms. We all have the obligation to eat the worms and eat the rot. We want an America where all of us play on an even playing field, by one set of rules.

**OPPOSITE
The Capitol
at dusk.
Photo by
Jim Belfon**

69

Why march? Father King said it was the shameful condition of the Negro. Today it's disgraceful.

Why do we march? Because our babies die earlier....

Why do we march? Because we're less able to get a primary or secondary education.

Why do we march? Because the media stereotypes us. We are projected as less intelligent than we are, less hardworking than we work, less universal than we are, less patriotic than we are, and more violent than we are.

Why do we march? We're less able to borrow money in a system built on credit and risk....

Why do we march? Because we're trapped in second-class schools and first-class jails.

What is the crisis? Wealth going upward, jobs going outward. Middle-class coming downward, the poor expanding rapidly.

Robert Sengstacke

The Reverend Jesse Jackson, Mayor Marion Barry, and New York City March Coordinator and radio host Bob Law (left) at the March.

Previous page: Reverend Jesse Jackson Photo by Brian Palmer

EXCERPTS FROM PRAYER DELIVERED AT THE MILLION MAN MARCH
BY ARCHBISHOP GEORGE A. STALLINGS

Take the hand of a brother next to you and let us bow our heads to pray.
To our God who was, before there even was a was!
And to our God who will be, when is and was are no more.
We come together in unity on this unprecedented historic day
on bended knee, acknowledging that we need Thee every hour.
God of our weary years, God of our silent tears, we admit
some of us have become so wrapped up, tied up, hooked up, and tangled up
in our own self-aggrandizement, self-centeredness, circumstance, and situation,
that some of us have forgotten you.

Not only have we forgotten that it was you who woke us up this
morning and started us on our way, but at times we have failed
to remember that it is in you that we live, move, and have our being.
For the time we have failed to remember that,
we ask to have your mercy and forgiveness.

**Archbishop
George A. Stallings**

Jason Miccolo Johnson

We, as proud Black men,
Black men from the rural South
and the industrial North,
we as struggling Black men,
from the heart of America
and the gleaming shores of the West,
we as accomplished Black men;
Black men from the East Coast
to the West Coast, have all sojourned
to this gateway of the Promised Land
to take ownership and control and lay claim
to our own destiny.
The daunting challenges are ever before us,
The opportunities for a brand-new
day are here.
Now is the acceptable time for
all that will be,
we say Yes!
Today is the hour of our salvation.
For all that will be, we say Yes!
For all that has been,
we are eternally grateful.

**Dr. Betty
Shabazz,
Mayor
Marion Barry,
and Cora
Masters Barry**

**Poet
Maya Angelou**

**Congressman
Charles Rangel**

Roy Lewis

Minister Louis Farrakhan,
the Reverend Willie Wilson,
the Reverend Ben Chavis,
and Mayor Marion Barry at
Union Temple Baptist Church.

Roy Lewis

The Reverend Al Sharpton and
activist Charles Baron.

8

MINISTER LOUIS FARRAKHAN

EXCERPTS FROM THE SPEECH OF MINISTER LOUIS FARRAKHAN

There's still two Americas—one black, one white, separate and unequal.
We're not here to tear down America. We're here to rebuild the wasted cities.

We, as a people, who have been fractured, divided, and destroyed because of our division, now must move toward a perfect union. And why did we come? We came because we want to move toward a more perfect union.

We cannot continue the destruction of our lives and the destruction of our community. But the change can't come until we feel sorry. There's a new Black man in America today, a new Black woman in America today.

We are talking about the moving toward a perfect union. Well, pointing out fault, pointing out our wrongs is the first step. The second step is to acknowledge. "Oh thank you. Oh, man, I'm wrong."

All of these Black men that the world sees as savage, maniacal, and bestial, look at them. A sea of peace. A sea of tranquillity.

Right here in this Mall where we are standing, according to books written on Washington, D.C., slaves used to be brought right here to this Mall in chains, to be sold up and down the eastern seaboard. Right along the Mall, going over to the White House, our fathers were sold into slavery.

Thomas Jefferson said he trembled for this country when he reflected that God was just and that his justice could not sleep forever.

Some of us are here because it's history making. Some of us are here because it's a march through which we can express anger and rage with America for what she has done and is doing to us. So we're here for many reasons. But the basic reason that this was called, was for atonement and reconciliation.

Black man, you don't have to bash White peoples. All we've got to do is go back home and turn our communities into productive places.

But every time we drive by shooting; every time we carjack; every time we use foul, filthy language; every time we produce culturally degenerate films and tapes,

75

putting a string in our women's backsides and parading them before the world; every time we do things like this we are feeding the degenerate mind of White supremacy.

We must become a totally organized people, and the way we can do that is to become a part of some organization that is working for the uplift of our people. Every one of you must go back and join a church, synagogue, temple, or mosque that is teaching spiritual and moral uplift.

There's no men in the church, in the mosque. The men are in the streets and we've got to get back to the houses of God. But preachers, we have to revive religion in America. We have to revive the houses of God, that they're not personal fiefdoms of those of us who are their preachers and pastors. We've got to be more like Jesus, more like Muhammad, more like Moses, and become servants of the people in fulfilling their needs.

Brothers, when you go home, we've got to register eight million eligible but unregistered brothers and sisters. So you go home and find eight more like yourself. You register them and get them to vote.

And then all of us can stand on the agenda. And in 1996, whoever the standard bearer is for the Democratic Party, the Republican Party, or the Independent Party, should one come into existence, they got to speak to our agenda. We are no longer going to vote for somebody just because they are Black. We've tried that. We wish we could. But we got to vote for you if you are compatible with our agenda.

And so we stand here today at this historic moment; we are standing in the place of those who could not make it here today. We are standing in the blood of our ancestors. We are standing on the blood of those who died in the middle passage, who died in the fields and swamps of America, who died hanging from trees in the South, who died in the cells of their jailers, who died on the highways and in the fratricidal conflict that rages within our community. We are standing on the sacrifice of the lives of those heroes, our great men and women, that we today may accept responsibility that life imposes upon each traveler who comes this way.

Minister Louis Farrakhan with his hands outstretched. Photo by Jason Miccolo Johnson

Now, brothers, moral and spiritual renewal is a necessity.

Minister Louis Farrakhan
with his son.

Fruit of Islam

9

THE PLEDGE

I pledge that from this day forward I will strive to love my brother as I love myself. I, from this day forward, will strive to improve myself spiritually, morally, mentally, socially, politically, and economically for the benefit of myself, my family, and my people. **I pledge** that I will strive to build businesses, build houses, build hospitals, build factories, and enter into international trade for the good of myself, my family, and my people.

I pledge that from this day forward I will never raise my hand with a knife or a gun to beat, cut, shoot any member of my family or any human being except in self-defense. **I pledge** from this day forward I will never abuse my wife by striking her, disrespecting her, for she is the mother of my children and the producer of my future. **I pledge** that from this day forward I will never engage in the abuse of children, little boys or little girls, for sexual gratification. For I will let them grow in peace to be strong men and women for the future of our people. I will never again use the B-word to describe any female—but particularly my own Black sister.

I pledge from this day forward that I will not poison my body with drugs or that which is destructive to my health and my well-being. **I pledge** from this day forward I will support Black newspapers, Black radio, Black television. I will support Black artists who clean up their act to show respect for their people and respect for the heirs of the human family.

I will do all of this, so help me God.

Photo by Lester Sloan

March participants
respond.

Jim Belfon

Bill O'Leary, The Washington Post

WE MARCH WITH THE
COURAGE OF SHAKA
THE DREAM OF MARTIN
THE LOVE OF JESUS
STRENGTH AND THE MILLION
OF A MEN

1,000,000 MEN 1 GOD

We march.

Power salute.

Voter registration.

10

THE FUTURE

Long live the spirit of the Million Man March!" the Black men chanted with pride, their clenched fists raised in the air. "Long live the spirit of the Million Man March!"

The invigorating refrain followed a solemn pledge uttered in unison by more than one million African-American men who stood shoulder to shoulder on the Mall in Washington, D.C., an oath for self-rehabilitation and self-respect. But after the euphoria wears off, after the speeches, poems, and prayers, after the Mall returns to an empty silence, there are hard questions that echo across America: What now? Where do African-American men go from here? How do Black men keep the spirit of the March alive? How do Black men cement the instinctive alliance that was forged during one fifteen-hour day? Will we work to rebuild our communities, provide unity within our families, join a church, and nurture young Black men who have lost their way?

Perhaps the answers to these questions can be found inside each one of us.

"We're already beginning to see evidence of Black men returning home, atoning and establishing a solid foundation for their families," said Conrad Muhammad. "I spoke with a sister who had not talked to her husband in two years. He had not made one single alimony payment, but after the March, she received a check for three thousand dollars. This is an example of the kind of goodwill that is taking place as a result of the Million Man March. There is more courtesy on the streets. This is the Lord's doing. Some of us have lost our way, we have not been involved in social movements after the sixties, drugs took up our time—but today there is a movement taking place; we'll see murder go down, we'll see robberies go down, and we'll begin to focus on each other. Minister Farrakhan asked us to go back to our towns and join a church or some religious organization, and we're already seeing a larger number of people joining these institutions. At our mosque, we had to put chairs outside the past weeks to handle the numbers. The Minister said that we don't have to reinvent the wheel, but to join organizations that already exist."

"We're getting reports that young Black men have gone back to their communities and have taken their pledge of working in their communities to heart," said the Reverend Benjamin Chavis. "They're joining organizations; they're talking about reducing Black-on-Black crime; they're setting up voter registration drives. The March was a transforming event, which is going to impact in a positive way on the lives of millions of African-American men who are carrying the spirit of the March with them."

"The first thing we do is remain bonded. We must join some group or

OPPOSITE
Michael Eric Dyson.
Photo by Eli Reed/ Magnum Photos

 83

church or mosque or organization whose teachings are in sync with our principles," said the Reverend Al Sharpton. "We must remain active and committed to bringing other Black men into the circle of commitment to voter registration, adopt children, and put aside time to volunteer to work in the community. We must make helping each other part of our existence, part of our lifestyle. I see this demonstration going way beyond the leaders who organized it—I see Black people organizing themselves."

Herb Boyd said the increased voter registration and, in turn, political power in the African-American community is likely to emerge as a result of the March. "The increased voter rolls, many pundits contend, could have an impact on state, city, and county legislative bodies," Boyd said. "Two days after the March, Minister Farrakhan intimated the possibility of forming an alternative force. He said, rather than establishing a third political power that will draw from the Democrats, the Republicans, and the Independents, we will work together. Should these plans cohere, it will mark the first time the Nation of Islam— which during the last decade, dropped its disavowal of electoral politics—has joined in a united-front effort or hinted at coalition politics. This political force driven by the Nation of Islam could alter the political landscape in the country."

"We must not let the message of the Million Man March be mangled by the discordant commentary that has surrounded it," the Reverend Jesse Jackson wrote in *The Los Angeles Times*.

"Hundreds of thousands of African-American men gathered together in a historic witness that confounded cynics. Their spirit was purposeful, not hostile. They found joy in unity, not division...As a minority against terrible odds, African-Americans have always known that political action grows out of personal responsibility, that pain must be turned to power."

Bob Law, nationally syndicated radio talk show host and March coordinator said, "It has created a new mindset that makes the rest of what has to be done possible. The principle on which the March was based is from the Bible... work on the renewal of your mind and all of you shall be redeemed."

"On a practical level, the self-examination and self-rehabilitation is something that must be taken seriously," said Michael Eric Dyson. "We must put into action a concrete application for higher ideals and responsible action. One can get involved in a local boys' club, work with the needy, there are many ways to become involved in the community, but the point is to translate that pledge of spirit to spiritual renewal. We have to translate that pledge into policing our communities, getting rid of crack houses, helping Black men who are displaced and who have slipped between the cracks, and helping them find gainful employment. We have to translate that euphoria and good feeling into something ongoing.

"Many of these men don't have the resources to behave decently. They have to endure financial assault and economic misery. They don't have the inspiration or the material or political means to be counted as worthwhile in our culture. So, unless the laws of the land are reshaped to bolster political and public policy to attend to those economic and social practices that harm Black men, the inspiration to act better may evaporate under the thick pressure of political resistance," Dyson said.

William Freeland, a Philadelphia bus driver, has been reaching out to save Black lives in his community for several years and said that as a result of the March, he is inspired to work even harder in the years to come.

Freeland's organization, Men Against Violence Network, was established five years ago after the death of a longtime friend. At the funeral, the men decided to meet once a month to discuss how to counsel young Black men on drugs, how to get young Black men off the streets and into productive jobs, how to prevent senseless acts of violence and death among African-American men in the Philadelphia area.

The network is composed of a number of Black men who were all gang members in the 1950s—men who know the temptations and evils of the street. "After talking about some of the negative things that we see in the community, we thought we had something to offer. We decided to try to bring kids back who were lost and misunderstood, and rebuild our communities. We've been working in the community for five years now and we'll be out there for many more."

Freeland said that he boarded one of twenty-four buses that rolled out of Philadelphia and explained that when they arrived at RFK Stadium, the men decided to walk to the Mall together—instead of riding the Metro—in a show of solidarity.

"It was about bonding with Black men, that's what this march was about for me," Freeland said. "We all walked together. It was such a beautiful thing. When I arrived and watched all the brothers hugging each other, it was just beautiful for me to see because I'm used to seeing brothers doing negative things."

Freeland said his group copied the definition for the word atonement and printed it on five hundred flyers that they passed out at the March. "We just wanted brothers to know exactly what it meant and what they were supposed to be doing."

The network has helped some Black men find shelter from the streets; they have taken up collections to pay for the funerals of men who had no families; they've helped clean up men on drugs; and they have adopted Paul Laurence Dunbar Elementary School in Philadelphia.

"When there is trouble in the community, when someone needs bodies, they get in touch with us and we get out into the neighborhoods and see if we can help," Freeland said. "God has a way of helping us, so we have to take care of our own."

Lester Sloan

FOI Profile.

Marchers clinging to a statue, chanting, "Be strong, Black man."

Healing unity to
move a nation.

Man in
uniform.

11

RANDOM ACTS OF BLACKNESS

All across America, African-American men have returned to their neighborhoods after the Million Man March with new life and a renewed commitment to improve the quality of their communities, block by block.

In Detroit, Black men jammed Fellowship Temple for a meeting several days after the March and signed up to adopt Black children and mentor teenagers after school.

In Philadelphia, members of a drug and alcohol rehabilitation program returned from Washington and spoke with young Black men about their responsibility as fathers and voters while another group of Black men used rakes and trash bags to clean up parks for children.

In Indianapolis, some Christian and Muslim ministers were joining forces for the first time to keep the spirit of the March alive in their community.

In Charlotte, there was a demonstration immediately after the Million Man March, which community leaders called "Stop the Killing."

On Long Island, New York, Randy Johnson interrupted his lunch to walk across a McDonald's restaurant to remind a group of young Black men who were yelling obscenities that their behavior in public perpetuates the negative stereotype of African-American men and is a reflection on all of us.

In Washington, Black men were seen lifting strollers over curbs for Black women who were pushing their babies along the sidewalk.

In Trenton, Black ministers were planning mini Marches to encourage voter registration and employment.

Philip Banks Jr., a retired police lieutenant from New York and his three sons, David, a lawyer, Terence, who has started his own business, and Philip III, a police officer, attended the March and told *Time* magazine that the family of men came away with a commitment to create a local, house-to-house voter registration drive.

I've seen a renewed sense of hope and pride in Black men since the Million Man March, Bishop Stallings said. Brothers are speaking to each other, they're calling each other ëbrother,' they're smiling at each other. I truly believe that Black men are feeling a deep sense of pride in being a Black man in America today, which did not exist prior to October 16. I believe there is a burning desire on the part of African-American men to improve the image of how White America views us; that we're not all on drugs, we're not all in jail; that we are committed, dedicated hardworking, responsible Black men who will provide leadership for our community and our nation.

Only we can heal our communities.

The answers to our problems are within us; within me, within you.

OPPOSITE
Congressman
Kweisi Mfume.
Photo by
Roy Lewis

 89

MILESTONES IN RESISTANCE AND SOLIDARITY: FROM SLAVE REVOLTS TO THE MILLION MAN MARCH

1526 - First recorded slave revolt at San Miguel de Gualdape in Virginia when African captives and Native Americans routed Spanish colonists.

1644 - Eleven Black servants of New Amsterdam, later New York City, filed a petition for freedom. The first legal protest in America.

1712 - A band of Black insurgents, planning to overthrow their oppressors, laid siege to New York City. They were captured and executed.

1811 - Between 300 and 500 slaves participated in the biggest slave rebellion in United States history in St. John the Baptist Parish, near New Orleans.

1843 - The National Negro Convention Movement, inaugurated in the 1830s, met in Buffalo, New York.

1850 - Harriet Tubman, having secured her own freedom, launched the first of many trips liberating some 300 slaves.

1863 - First extensive combat by African-American troops in the Civil War took place at Port Hudson and Milliken's Bend, near Vicksburg, Mississippi.

1898 - Journalist T. Thomas Fortune organized the Afro-American Council, called the first American civil rights organization.

1909 - Seeking an end to racial prjudice, W.E.B. DuBois and other activists formed the National Association for the Advancement of Colored People (NAACP).

1920 - Thousands attend the annual Universal Negro Improvement Association (UNIA) convention at Madison Square Garden to hear its leader, Marcus Garvey, talk about African redemption.

1934 - The Honorable Elijah Muhammad succeeds W. D. Fard as leader of the Nation of Islam.

1941 - A threatened march on Washington, led by labor activists A. Philip Randolph and Bayard Rustin, forces President Franklin D. Roosevelt to sign an executive order to integrate the defense industry.

1947 - To test the Supreme Court's ban against segregation in interstate bus travel, theCongress of Racial Equality (CORE) sends the first wave of Freedom Riders to the South.

1955 - When Rosa Parks refuses to relinquish her seat and move to the back of the bus, her action sparks the Montgomery Bus Boycott.

1961 - Hundreds turn out each week on the streets of Harlem to hear Malcolm X lecture on the evils of White supremacy.

1963 - The largest protest demonstration in the nation's history assembled at the Lincoln Memorial in Washington, D.C. More than 250,000 people heard Dr. Martin Luther King, Jr., deliver his famous "*I Have a Dream*" speech.

1966 - Huey Newton and Bobby Seale founded the Black Panther Party in Oakland, California.

1967 - H. Rap Brown is appointed the new chairman of the Student Nonviolent Coordinating Committee (SNCC), replacing Stokely Carmichael.

1968 - In May, the Reverend Ralph Abernathy led nin caravans of poor people to Washington, D.C., as part of the first phase of the Poor People's Campaign. Second Black Power Conference is held in Philadelphia in June.

1969 - One hundred students seized the Student Union Building at Cornell University to protest university racism.

1974 - Approximately five hundred delegates and observers, almost half of them from America, attended the Sixth Pan-African Congress in Dar es Salaam, Tanzania.

1981 - More than 300,000 demonstrators from labor and civil rights organizations protested the social policies of the Reagan administration in Solidarity Day march in Washington, D.C.

1992 - The acquittal of White police officers in Los Angeles, charged with beating Rodney King, sparked the most severe race riot in U.S. history. In the three days of rioting, 58 people were killed and property damage was estimated at $550 million.

1995 - With an aim toward personal atonement, more than a million Black men answered Minister Louis Farrakhan's call to march in Washington, D.C. It is the largest assembly of Black people in the nation's history.

Compiled by Herb Boyd

RESOURCES

The following is a sampling of some of the organizations and programs available to assist you in carrying out the message of the Million Man March. Please check your local directory for organizations and programs in your community.

NATIONAL

A Better Chance
419 Boylston Street
Boston, MA 02116
617-421-0950

Black Business Alliance
P.O. Box 26443
Baltimore, MD 21207
410-467-7427

Black Veterans
686 Fulton Street
Brooklyn, NY 11217
718-935-1116

Center for Constitutional Rights
666 Broadway
New York, NY 10012
212-614-6464

Coalition of Black Trade Unionists
P.O. Box 73120
Washington, DC 20056-3120
202-429-1203

NAACP
260 Fifth Avenue
New York, NY 10003
212-481-4100

National Black United Fund
50 Park Place
Newark, NJ 07102
201-643-5122

National Black Survival Fund
P.O. Box 3005
Lafayette, LA 70502
318-232-7672

National Black Leadership Council
250 West 54th Street
New York, NY 10019
212-541-7600

National Minority Business Council
235 East 42nd Street
New York, NY 10017
212-573-2385

National Prison Project
1875 Connecticut Avenue, NW
Washington, DC 20009
202-234-4830

Operation PUSH
930 East 50th Street
Chicago, IL 60615
312-373-3366

National Urban League, Inc.
500 East 62nd Street
New York, NY
212-310-9000

YOUTH

Children's Defense Fund
25 E Street, NW
Washington, DC 20001
202-628-8787

National Association of Police Athletic
   Leagues
200 Castlewood Drive
North Palm Beach, FL 33408
407-884-1823

National Youth Employment Coalition
1001 Connecticut Avenue, NW
Washington, DC 20009
202-659-1064

National Black Youth Leadership Council
250 West 54th Street
New York, NY 10019
212-541-7600

Advocates for Youth
1025 Vermont Avenue, NW
Washington, DC 20005
202-347-5700

Big Brother and Big Sister of America
230 North 13th Street
Philadelphia, PA 19107
215-567-7000

Boys and Girls Clubs of America
1230 West Peach Street, NW
Atlanta, GA 30309-3447
404-815-5700

YMCA
101 North Wacker Drive
Chicago, IL 60606
312-977-0031

The Rosa and Raymond Parks Institute
   for Self Development
65 Cadillac Square
Detroit, MI 48226
313-965-0606

City Kids Foundation
57 Leonard Street
New York, NY 10013
212-925-3320

Girls, Inc.
30 East 33rd Street
New York, NY 10016
212-689-3700

Jackie Robinson Foundation
3 West 35th Street
New York, NY 10001
212-290-8600

I Have a Dream Foundation
300 Seventh Avenue
New York, NY 10001
212-736-1730

ADOPTION

Spence-Chapin
6 East 94th Street
New York, NY 10128
212-369-0300

Black Adoption Consortium
5090 Central Highway #6
Pennsauken, NJ 08109
609-486-0100

Black Adoption Placement
506 15th Street
Oakland, CA 94612
510-839-3678

Black Adoption Services of Three Rivers
307 Fourth Avenue
Pittsburgh, PA 15222
412-471-8722

Black Family and Children's Services
2323 North Third Street
Phoenix, AZ 85004
602-256-2948

Harambee Services to Black Families
1468 East 55th Street
Cleveland, OH 44103
216-391-7044

Harlem Downing Children's Services
2090 Adam Clayton Powell Blvd.
New York, NY 10027
212-749-3656

Homes for Black Children
2340 Calvert
Detroit, MI 48206
313-869-2316

Homes for Black Children
3131 East 38th Street
Indianapolis, IN 46218
317-545-5281

Institute for Black Parenting
9920 La Cienega Blvd.
Inglewood, CA 90301
310-348-1400
800-367-8858

North Carolina Friends of Black Children
610 West Main Street
Sanford, NC 27330
919-733-9296

Tayarl African-American
11011 Scripps Ranch Boulevard
San Diego, CA 92131
619-266-6066

OTHER SERVICES

Al-Anon Family Group Headquarters
P.O. Box 862, Midtown Station
New York, NY 10018
212-302-7240

Phoenix House Foundation
164 West 74th Street
New York, NY 10023
212-595-5810

National Minority AIDS Council
300 Eye Street NE
Washington, DC 20002
202-544-1072

▲ Author Michael Cottman
(right) with friends.
Photo by Josanne Lopez

PREVIOUS PAGES
The Mall.
Photo by Harlee Little

Ron Campbell

Actor
T.C. Carter

Winston Kennedy

Activist/author
Sam Anderson

Fruit of Islam on steps of Canadian
Embassy, Washington, D.C.

Minister Louis Farrakhan

**Congressman Donald Payne
Congressional Black Caucus
Photo by Lester Sloan**

ACKNOWLEDGMENTS

I would first like to thank the organizers of the Million Man March, for without this profound, mass meeting of African-American men that unfolded before the world, there would be no words for me to write, no images for these photographers to capture.

A debt of thanks to Minister Louis Farrakhan for his vision; The Nation of Islam Minister Conrad Muhammad, head of Mosque number 7, New York City; the Reverend Benjamin Chavis; Dr. Cornel West; the Reverend Jesse Jackson; the Reverend Al Sharpton; the ministers of all denominations who came together to make this March, this movement, a spiritual foundation for each of us to stand upon.

Thanks to each of the gifted photographers whose powerful images will remain with us when we close our eyes in the evenings; to my publisher, Adrienne Ingrum, whose constant reminder that African-American people must tell our own stories made this book possible; to Richard Myers and everyone at The Crown Publishing Group, for their support and kindness; to Hilary Bass for taking all of my telephone calls. Thanks to Bob Slade and Ann Tripp and everyone at WRKS-FM in New York City.

To my true friends, whose love, support, advice, and humor I've come to depend on, thank you so much: Monte R. Young, Michael Tucker, Kevin Merida, and Nick Chiles, for your contributions and insight; to Steve Bacon, Larry Bivins, Neil Foote, Lee May, and Clem Richardson, for being brothers in spirit; to Dr. Jose Jones, Thomas Finlayson, Andrew Rhoden, and the National Association of Black Scuba Divers for being dive buddies for life; to Hank Jennings and Eugene Niles, my partners for the Million Man March, my comrades on shore, and my soulmates beneath the sea. Thank you, Pam Newkirk and Felicia Lee, for underscoring the importance of creative independence. Thank you Wilbert Bacon, not only for your wise words for this book, but for your constant guidance the past 30 years. Thank you, Lamar and Diane Gatewood, for being patient with me.

Thank you, Josanne Lopez, for reminding me that we must always thank our African ancestors, our Black forefathers who came before us; thank you for your support, kindness and television tutoring. Thank you for your contribution to this book and being a true touchstone.

To Marie Dutton Brown, my literary agent, my spiritual and intellectual counselor, my friend. If I used all the pages that I felt necessary to truly thank you for everything you've done for me, every inch of the twenty-two block Mall in Washington, D.C., would be littered with paper. Because of you, I am a better writer, a better thinker, a better person.

We all thank our extraordinary editorial and production team, whose long hours, talent, professionalism is acknowledged and greatly appreciated. Thank you Linda Tarrant-Reid, Managing Editor, who kept it all together and flowing, her support staff, Donna Middleton Spalter, Karen Taylor, and design and production team, Péju Alawusa and Kelvin Oden.

Thanks to my family; Aunt Patricia, I love you; to Howard and Evelyn House in Detroit; Aunt Faustina Pryor and family in Indianapolis; to Aunt Annie, Laurie Davis in California; to Eddie and Jean Favors (Jean, thanks for being there when I get blocked); to Aunt Rose and the Vanderlips in New Rochelle, New York; to Joan and David Thomas; to Liz and Randy Johnson; to Harry and Eugene Grangenois; to Tom Banks.

To my wife, Mireille, who keeps me focused, who challenges me to dig deep, who I lean on for strength, who comforts my soul and reminds me that God is my true spiritual compass. I love you.

Thank you, Mother and Father, Roberta and Howard Cottman, for your love, devotion, and direction over my 39 years; thank you for all the books by Black writers, for teaching me about the Black experience in America, and for taking me through tours of African-American history museums when I was too young to appreciate the big picture. You both have instilled within me a passion for my people in ways that I discover anew each time I sit down to set words to a blank page.

I love you both.

—Michael Cottman

Thank you to the following individuals for their support and assistance: Michel DuCille, Elanna Haywood, Sharon Howard, Steven Newsome, Suzanne Pilet, Shirley Solomon, Mark Wright, Shireen Dodson, Jane Lusaka, and Winston Kennedy.

—Deborah Willis